# Mastering Your Money: A Comprehensive Guide to Personal Finance

## Vana Hendy

ISBN:9798878879286

# DEDICATION

With the help of Almighty God who lives forever,I dedicate this work to all who sees the need to do the right thing at the right time;YOU.

# CONTENTS

# ACKNOWLEDGMENTS

I would like to express my heartfelt gratitude to the individuals who have played a significant role in the realization of this book. Their support, guidance, and encouragement have been invaluable.

First and foremost, I extend my deepest thanks to Almighty God for his love and mercy,I also want to thank my family and friends for their expertise, inspiration, encouragement.Your wisdom, insights, motivation significantly enriched this project.

I am also grateful to My Lecturers for their editorial assistance, feedback, support during challenging times.Your keen eye and thoughtful suggestions have greatly enhanced the quality of this work.

A special thanks to my mentor for his technical assistance and research support. Your dedication and expertise were instrumental in bringing this book to fruition.

Finally, a heartfelt thank you to my readers.

Your interest in my work is the ultimate reward, and I am truly grateful for the opportunity to share this story with you.

Thank you all for being a part of this journey.

Sincerely,


Vana Hendy.

# 1 BUILDING A FOUNDATION FOR FINANCIAL SUCCESS

In the vast landscape of personal finance, establishing a solid foundation is the key to unlocking a future of financial abundance and security. As you embark on this journey to master your money, it's crucial to recognize the importance of laying down a strong groundwork that will support your financial goals and aspirations.

## Understanding Your Financial Landscape

Before we delve into the intricacies of budgeting, saving, and investing, let's take a moment to survey the terrain of your personal finances. Like a skilled cartographer mapping uncharted territories, you must familiarize yourself with the various elements that make up your financial landscape.

Income Streams: Identify and evaluate all

sources of income, including your primary job, side hustles, investments, and any passive income streams. Understanding the dynamics of your income is fundamental to crafting a sustainable financial plan.

Expenses Inventory: Conduct a thorough examination of your monthly expenses. Categorize them into fixed (mortgage or rent, utilities) and variable (groceries, entertainment). This will provide a clear picture of where your money is going and where potential savings can be made.

Debt Assessment: Take stock of any outstanding debts, such as student loans, credit card balances, or car loans. Knowing your debt situation is crucial for developing effective strategies to manage and eliminate these financial obligations.

**Setting Financial Goals**
With a clear understanding of your financial landscape, the next step is to set actionable and realistic financial goals. Whether your objectives involve saving for a down payment on a house, starting an emergency fund, or planning for retirement, establishing clear

goals will serve as your financial compass.

Short-Term Goals: These are objectives you aim to achieve within the next 1-2 years, such as creating an emergency fund, paying off high-interest debt, or saving for a vacation.

Medium-Term Goals: Spanning 3-5 years, medium-term goals might include saving for a home, funding your child's education, or starting a business.

Long-Term Goals: Consider your aspirations for the next 10, 20, or even 30 years. This could involve retirement planning, substantial investments, or leaving a financial legacy for future generations.

**Embracing Financial Literacy**
In the realm of personal finance, knowledge is indeed power. Embracing financial literacy is akin to equipping yourself with a robust set of tools and strategies that will enable you to navigate the complex landscape of money management with confidence and clarity.

Educate Yourself: Take advantage of the plethora of resources available to enhance your financial literacy. From books and online courses to podcasts and seminars, there are countless avenues to deepen your understanding of topics such as investing, retirement planning, and tax optimization.

keep Up: The banking industry is a dynamic, e ver-changing field.Stay abreast of current events, economic trends, and legislative changes that may impact your financial situation. Being informed allows you to make proactive decisions and adapt your financial strategies accordingly.

Seek Professional Guidance: Don't hesitate to seek guidance from financial professionals such as certified financial planners, investment advisors, or tax specialists. These experts can provide personalized advice tailored to your specific needs and goals, helping you make informed decisions that align with your long-term objectives.

**Cultivating Financial Discipline**
Discipline is the bedrock upon which financial success is built. Cultivating healthy financial habits and exercising restraint in your spending and saving behaviors are essential

components of achieving your long-term financial goals.

Live Below Your Means: Adopt a lifestyle that allows you to live comfortably within your means while leaving room for savings and investments. Avoid succumbing to lifestyle inflation and the temptation to overspend when your income increases.

Practice Delayed Gratification: Learn to differentiate between needs and wants, and prioritize your spending accordingly. Embrace the concept of delayed gratification by deferring unnecessary purchases in favor of long-term financial security and stability.

Automate Your Finances: Leverage technology to streamline your financial management processes and eliminate the risk of missed payments or oversights. Set up automatic transfers to savings accounts, automate bill payments, and utilize budgeting apps to track your spending in real-time.

## Building Resilience and Adaptability
In an unpredictable world fraught with economic uncertainty and unforeseen

challenges, building resilience and adaptability are essential qualities for safeguarding your financial well-being.

Establish an Emergency Fund: Life is replete with unexpected emergencies and financial setbacks. Establishing an emergency fund with 3-6 months' worth of living expenses can provide a financial safety net to weather unforeseen circumstances without derailing your long-term goals.

Diversify Your Income Streams: Relying solely on a single source of income leaves you vulnerable to economic fluctuations and job insecurity. Explore opportunities to diversify your income streams through side hustles, passive investments, or freelance work to enhance your financial stability and resilience.

**Unveiling the Psychology of Money**
Understanding the psychology behind financial decisions is a pivotal aspect of mastering personal finance. Our attitudes, beliefs, and behaviors regarding money play a significant role in shaping our financial outcomes. Delving into the psychological nuances of finance can empower you to make

informed decisions and establish a healthy mindset towards wealth.

Money Mindset: Reflect on your beliefs and attitudes towards money. Whether you view money as a tool
for empowerment, security, or as a source of stress can significantly impact your financial choices. Cultivating a positive money mindset can foster a healthy relationship with your finances and contribute to your overall well-being.

Identifying and Overcoming Money Blocks: Uncover any deep-seated beliefs or fears that may be hindering your financial progress. Whether it's a fear of scarcity, a reluctance to invest, or an aversion to discussing money, addressing and overcoming these money blocks is crucial for unlocking your full financial potential.

Goal Visualization: Picture your financial goals vividly. Visualization can serve as a powerful motivator, helping you stay focused on your objectives. Envision the lifestyle you aspire to, the experiences you want to enjoy, and the impact you wish to make through your financial journey.

## Navigating the Credit Landscape

Credit is a double-edged sword that, when wielded wisely, can open doors to opportunities, yet mismanagement can lead to financial pitfalls. Understanding the intricacies of credit is essential for building a strong financial foundation.

Credit Scores and Reports: Familiarize yourself with the components of credit scores and regularly monitor your credit reports. A good credit score is crucial for obtaining favorable interest rates on loans, securing rental agreements, and even landing certain jobs. Be proactive in addressing any discrepancies on your credit report.

Responsible Credit Card Usage: Credit cards offer convenience, rewards, and the opportunity to build credit. However, it's imperative to use them responsibly. Avoid accumulating high balances, pay your bills on time, and take advantage of rewards programs without succumbing to unnecessary debt.

Strategic Debt Management: Not all debt is

detrimental, but managing it strategically is key. Distinguish between "good" debt, such as a mortgage or student loans, and "bad" debt, like high-interest credit card balances. Develop a plan to pay off high-interest debt systematically while leveraging low-interest debt for wealth-building opportunities.

## Maximizing Income and Investment Potential

Increasing your income and strategically investing your money are essential components of financial mastery. Explore avenues to optimize your earning potential and make informed investment decisions aligned with your goals.

Continuous Skill Development: Invest in your skills and education to enhance your earning potential. Acquiring new qualifications or honing existing talents can open doors to career advancement and income growth.

Smart Investing Strategies: Understand the various investment vehicles available and tailor your investment strategy to align with your risk tolerance, time horizon, and financial goals. Whether it's stocks, bonds, real estate, or retirement accounts, a diversified portfolio can mitigate risk and enhance long-term returns.

Tax Optimization: Explore tax-efficient strategies to maximize your income and minimize tax liabilities. Leveraging tax-advantaged accounts, deductions, and credits can significantly impact your overall financial picture.

As you continue your journey toward mastering personal finance, remember that each chapter unfolds new opportunities for growth and learning. By delving into the psychology of money, navigating the credit landscape, and maximizing income and investment potential, you equip yourself with a holistic understanding of the multifaceted world of personal finance. In the upcoming chapters, we will delve into more advanced strategies and practical tips to further enhance your financial acumen.

# 2 THE ART OF BUDGETING: A BLUEPRINT FOR FINANCIAL SUCCESS

Budgeting is the cornerstone of effective financial management, providing a roadmap to guide your spending, saving, and investing decisions. In this chapter, we will delve into the art of budgeting, exploring practical strategies to create and maintain a budget that aligns with your financial goals and aspirations.

## Understanding the Purpose of Budgeting

At its core, budgeting is about more than just tracking expenses; it's about taking control of your financial destiny. By creating a budget, you gain insight into your income and expenditures, identify areas where you can trim expenses, and allocate resources towards achieving your financial objectives.

Income Assessment: Begin by calculating your total monthly income from all sources, including wages, salaries, bonuses, and any other sources of revenue. Understanding your income stream is the foundation upon which your budget will be built.

Expense Evaluation: Next, scrutinize your monthly expenses across various categories, such as housing, transportation, groceries, entertainment, and debt repayments. Be thorough in your assessment, accounting for both fixed expenses (e.g., rent, utilities) and variable expenses (e.g., dining out, shopping).

Goal Alignment: Once you have a clear understanding of your income and expenses, align your budget with your financial goals. Allocate funds towards savings, debt repayment, investments, and discretionary spending in accordance with your priorities and aspirations.

## Creating Your Budget

With a clear understanding of your financial landscape and objectives, it's time to create your budget. While there are numerous budgeting methods and tools available, the key is to find a approach that resonates with your preferences and lifestyle.

Traditional Budgeting: The traditional approach involves categorizing your income and expenses into predefined categories and setting spending limits for each category. Tools such as spreadsheets or budgeting apps can streamline the process and provide insights into your spending patterns.

Zero-Based Budgeting: In zero-based budgeting, every dollar of income is allocated towards specific expenses, savings, or investments, leaving no room for unallocated funds. This method encourages conscious decision-making and ensures that every dollar serves a purpose.

Envelope System: The envelope system involves allocating cash into physical envelopes labeled with different expense categories. Once an envelope is empty, spending in that category must cease until the next budgeting period. This method provides a tangible representation of your budget and helps prevent overspending.

## Staying on Track

Creating a budget is only the first step; maintaining it requires diligence, discipline, and periodic reassessment. Here are some strategies to help you stay on track with your budgeting goals:

Regular Review: Review your budget regularly to track your progress, identify any deviations from your plan, and make adjustments as needed. Life circumstances, income fluctuations, and unexpected expenses may necessitate modifications to your budget over time.

Emergency Fund: Build an emergency fund to cushion against unforeseen financial setbacks and prevent them from derailing your budget. Aim to set aside 3-6 months' worth of living expenses in a liquid, accessible account to provide a financial safety net.

Flexibility and Adaptability: Be flexible and adaptable in your budgeting approach. While it's important to stick to your financial plan, recognize that unexpected expenses or opportunities may arise that require adjustments to your budgeting priorities.

## Fine-Tuning Your Budgeting Skills

As you continue on your journey toward financial mastery, fine-tuning your budgeting skills becomes increasingly important. Here are some advanced strategies to help you optimize your budget and maximize your financial potential:

Expense Tracking: Dive deeper into your spending habits by meticulously tracking every expense. Utilize budgeting apps or spreadsheets to categorize expenditures and identify areas where you can cut back or reallocate funds. Analyzing your spending patterns allows for more precise budget adjustments and greater control over your finances.

Budget Variability: Recognize that not all expenses are fixed; some fluctuate from month to month. Incorporate variability into your budgeting approach by allocating a range rather than a fixed amount for certain expenses, such as groceries or utilities. This flexibility accommodates fluctuations in spending while maintaining overall budget integrity.

Sinking Funds: Anticipate irregular or infrequent expenses, such as annual insurance premiums or holiday gifts, by setting up sinking funds. Allocate a portion of your budget towards these expenses each month, building up a reserve to cover the costs when they arise. Sinking funds prevent large expenses from derailing your budget and provide peace of mind knowing that you're adequately prepared.

Trimming Expenses: Continuously seek opportunities to trim unnecessary expenses and optimize your spending. Evaluate subscription services, negotiate bills, and seek out discounts or promotional offers to reduce costs without sacrificing quality of life. Every dollar saved can be redirected towards your financial goals, accelerating your progress towards financial independence.

### Advanced Budgeting Techniques
Explore advanced budgeting techniques to further enhance your financial management skills and achieve greater efficiency and effectiveness in your budgeting process:

Incremental Budgeting: Instead of creating a new budget from scratch each month, employ an incremental approach by building upon the previous month's budget. Adjust allocations based on changing circumstances, goals, and priorities while maintaining a consistent framework. Incremental budgeting streamlines the budgeting process and fosters continuity and consistency over time.

Forecasting: Project future income and expenses based on historical data, anticipated changes, and upcoming events. By forecasting your financial outlook, you can proactively plan for future expenses, identify potential challenges, and make preemptive adjustments to your budget. Forecasting provides a forward-looking perspective, enabling you to stay ahead of financial curveballs and capitalize on emerging opportunities.

Scenario Planning: Anticipate various financial scenarios and develop contingency plans to mitigate risks and capitalize on opportunities. Whether it's a job loss, medical emergency, or market downturn, scenario planning allows you to prepare for potential disruptions and adapt your budget accordingly. By considering multiple outcomes and planning for contingencies, you empower yourself to navigate uncertainties with confidence and resilience.

## Integrating Technology and Automation

Harness the power of technology and automation to streamline your budgeting process and optimize your financial management efforts:

Budgeting Apps: Leverage budgeting apps and software to automate expense tracking, categorization, and budget monitoring. These tools offer real-time insights into your financial health, provide personalized recommendations, and facilitate seamless coordination across multiple financial accounts.

Automatic Transfers: Automate savings contributions, debt repayments, and investment allocations by setting up automatic transfers. Schedule recurring transfers to designated accounts, ensuring that your financial priorities are consistently funded without the need for manual intervention.

Alerts and Notifications: Configure alerts and notifications to stay informed about significant financial events, such as low account balances, upcoming bills, or irregular spending patterns. These notifications serve as timely reminders and prompts for proactive financial management actions, helping you stay on top of your budgeting goals.

By incorporating advanced budgeting techniques, embracing technology and automation, and continuously refining your budgeting skills, you can optimize your financial management efforts and accelerate your journey toward financial freedom and prosperity.

### Building a Budgeting Community

While personal finance is, by its nature, a personal endeavor, building a supportive community can significantly enhance your budgeting journey. Surround yourself with like-minded individuals who share similar financial goals and values, whether it's joining online forums, participating in local meetups, or forming accountability groups with friends or family members. A budgeting community provides encouragement, accountability, and valuable insights, fostering a collaborative environment where members can learn from each other's experiences and celebrate successes together.

## Embracing Mindful Spending

Incorporate mindfulness into your spending habits by cultivating awareness and intentionality in your financial decisions. Before making a purchase, pause and consider whether it aligns with your values, priorities, and long-term goals. Practicing mindful spending encourages conscious consumption, reduces impulse purchases, and fosters a deeper appreciation for the things that truly matter in life. By aligning your spending with your values and aspirations, you can derive greater satisfaction and fulfillment from your financial choices while staying true to your budgeting principles.

## Cultivating Financial Resilience

In an ever-changing economic landscape, cultivating financial resilience is essential for weathering unforeseen challenges and uncertainties. Diversify your income streams, build multiple sources of revenue, and develop alternative income streams such as freelance work, rental income, or passive investments. Additionally, prioritize building a robust emergency fund to provide a financial buffer against unexpected expenses or income disruptions. By proactively preparing for potential setbacks and building resilience into your financial plan, you can navigate turbulent times with confidence and peace of mind.

### Practicing Gratitude and Abundance

Shift your mindset from scarcity to abundance by cultivating gratitude for the resources and opportunities available to you. Take time to appreciate the progress you've made on your budgeting journey, celebrate small victories, and express gratitude for the abundance in your life, whether it's financial stability, supportive relationships, or personal growth. Practicing gratitude fosters a positive outlook, reduces stress, and reinforces the belief that there is always enough to go around. By embracing abundance mentality, you can attract more opportunities for prosperity and abundance into your life, further enriching your financial well-being.

### Reflecting on Your Financial Journey

Finally, take time to reflect on your financial journey periodically. Celebrate how far you've come, acknowledge the challenges you've overcome, and recalibrate your goals and priorities as needed. Reflective practice allows you to gain perspective, learn from past experiences, and make informed decisions moving forward. Whether it's journaling about your financial wins and lessons learned or engaging in regular financial check-ins with yourself or a trusted advisor, introspection plays a crucial role in sustaining long-term financial success and fulfillment.

As you continue on your budgeting journey, remember that it's not just about balancing numbers; it's about cultivating a mindset of empowerment, intentionality, and abundance. By building a supportive community, embracing mindful spending, cultivating financial resilience, practicing gratitude, and reflecting on your financial journey, you can unlock the true potential of budgeting as a tool for personal growth and fulfillment. In the subsequent chapters, we will delve into additional topics to further empower you on your path to financial mastery.

# 3 MASTERING SAVING STRATEGIES: BUILDING YOUR FINANCIAL FORTRESS

Saving money is the cornerstone of financial stability and long-term wealth accumulation. In this chapter, we will explore various saving strategies and techniques to help you build a solid financial foundation, achieve your short-term and long-term goals, and secure your financial future.

**Setting Savings Goals**
Before diving into specific saving strategies, it's essential to establish clear and achievable savings goals. Whether you're saving for an emergency fund, a down payment on a house, a dream vacation, or retirement, defining your objectives provides focus and motivation for your saving efforts.

SMART Goals: Utilize the SMART criteria—specific, measurable, achievable, relevant, and time-bound—to set meaningful savings goals. Break down larger goals into smaller, actionable steps, and assign deadlines to track progress effectively.

Emergency Fund: Prioritize building an emergency fund to cover unexpected expenses, such as medical emergencies, car repairs, or job loss. Aim to save at least three to six months' worth of living expenses in a liquid, easily accessible account to provide a financial safety net in times of need.

Short-Term Goals: Identify short-term savings goals, such as saving for a vacation, purchasing a new vehicle, or funding home improvements. Allocate a portion of your budget towards these goals each month and track your progress to ensure timely achievement.

Long-Term Goals: Plan for your long-term financial objectives, such as retirement, education funding, or wealth accumulation. Consider employing tax-advantaged accounts, such as IRAs or 401(k)s, to maximize growth potential and minimize tax liabilities over time.

## Implementing Saving Strategies

With your savings goals established, it's time to implement effective saving strategies to reach them efficiently and sustainably. Explore the following strategies to optimize your saving efforts and accelerate your progress towards financial independence:

Pay Yourself First: Adopt the "pay yourself first" principle by prioritizing savings before allocating funds to discretionary expenses. Set up automatic transfers to designated savings accounts immediately after receiving your paycheck to ensure consistent and disciplined saving habits.

Budgeting for Savings: Treat savings as a non-negotiable expense in your budget, alongside essential living expenses such as housing, utilities, and groceries. Allocate a predetermined percentage of your income towards savings each month, and adjust your spending accordingly to accommodate your savings goals.

Tracking Expenses: Monitor your spending habits closely to identify areas where you can cut back and redirect funds towards savings. Utilize budgeting apps or spreadsheets to track expenses in real-time, analyze spending patterns, and identify opportunities for cost-saving measures.

Automating Savings: Leverage automation tools and features offered by banks and financial institutions to streamline your saving process. Set up recurring transfers or automatic contributions to savings accounts, investment accounts, or retirement accounts to ensure consistent saving habits without the need for manual intervention.

## Maximizing Saving Opportunities

In addition to traditional saving strategies, explore alternative avenues to maximize saving opportunities and accelerate your progress towards your financial goals:

Employer-Sponsored Retirement Plans: Take advantage of employer-sponsored retirement plans, such as 401(k)s or 403(b)s, if available. Contribute enough to qualify for employer matching contributions, if offered, to maximize the benefits of employer-sponsored retirement savings.

Health Savings Accounts (HSAs) and Flexible Spending Accounts (FSAs): If eligible, contribute to health savings accounts (HSAs) or flexible spending accounts (FSAs) to save for qualified medical expenses on a tax-advantaged basis. Maximize contributions to these accounts to reduce out-of-pocket healthcare costs and increase your overall savings potential.

High-Yield Savings Accounts: Explore high-yield savings accounts offered by online banks or financial institutions to earn higher interest rates on your savings compared to traditional savings accounts. Research and compare options to find accounts that offer competitive interest rates and minimal fees to maximize your savings potential.

Debt Reduction: Prioritize debt reduction as a form of saving by allocating extra funds towards paying down high-interest debt. By reducing debt balances, you free up future cash flow for savings and investments, accelerate your progress towards financial independence, and minimize interest expenses over time.

## Monitoring Progress and Adjusting Strategies

Regularly monitor your saving progress and adjust your strategies as needed to stay on track towards your financial goals. Track your savings contributions, review your budget regularly, and reassess your savings goals periodically to ensure alignment with changing circumstances or priorities. Celebrate milestones and achievements along the way, and remain flexible and adaptable in your approach to saving to optimize your financial outcomes over time.

By implementing effective saving strategies, maximizing saving opportunities, and monitoring progress closely, you can build a solid financial foundation, achieve your short-term and long-term goals, and secure your financial future. In the subsequent chapters, we will explore additional topics such as debt management, investment principles, and wealth-building strategies to further enhance your financial acumen and empower you on your journey towards financial mastery.

### Advanced Saving Techniques

As you delve deeper into the realm of saving, consider implementing advanced techniques to optimize your saving potential and maximize your financial resources:

Lifestyle Adjustments: Evaluate your lifestyle and identify areas where you can make meaningful adjustments to increase your saving capacity. Consider downsizing your living space, minimizing discretionary expenses, or exploring alternative transportation options to free up additional funds for saving.

Cash Windfalls: Capitalize on unexpected cash windfalls, such as tax refunds, bonuses, or inheritances, by directing a significant portion towards savings. Rather than succumbing to lifestyle inflation, use windfall money strategically to accelerate progress towards your savings goals and enhance your financial security.

Tax Optimization: Explore tax-efficient saving strategies to minimize tax liabilities and maximize savings potential. Contribute to tax-advantaged accounts, such as individual retirement accounts (IRAs) or health savings accounts (HSAs), to benefit from tax deductions or tax-free growth on your savings. Consult with a tax advisor to identify opportunities for tax optimization tailored to your financial situation.

Periodic Savings Challenges: Challenge yourself to periodic savings challenges to boost motivation and momentum towards your savings goals. Whether it's a no-spend month, a savings sprint to reach a specific milestone, or a savings competition with friends or family members, incorporating gamification into your saving efforts can inject fun and excitement into the process.

## Harnessing the Power of Compound Interest

Embrace the power of compound interest as a potent wealth-building tool to accelerate your saving efforts and achieve exponential growth over time. Compound interest allows your savings to grow not only on the principal amount but also on the accumulated interest, leading to accelerated growth potential over the long term.

Start Early: The earlier you start saving and investing, the more time your money has to compound and grow. Even small contributions made consistently over time can accumulate into significant wealth due to the compounding effect.

Consistent Contributions: Maintain consistent contributions to your savings and investment accounts to maximize the benefits of compound interest. Automate contributions to your retirement accounts, investment portfolios, or other savings vehicles to ensure regular and disciplined saving habits.

Reinvestment of Earnings: Reinvest dividends, interest, and capital gains earned from your investments to further amplify the power of compound interest. Rather than withdrawing earnings, allow them to compound over time, increasing your overall investment returns and accelerating wealth accumulation.

Long-Term Perspective: Adopt a long-term perspective when harnessing the power of compound interest. While market fluctuations may occur in the short term, staying invested and committed to your saving and investment goals allows you to capitalize on the compounding effect and achieve significant wealth accumulation over time.

## Leveraging Saving Milestones

Celebrate saving milestones along your financial journey as markers of progress and achievements. Whether it's reaching a specific savings target, achieving a certain investment milestone, or surpassing a personal savings record, acknowledging and celebrating these milestones reinforces positive saving habits and motivates continued progress towards your financial goals.

Milestone Rewards: Reward yourself for reaching saving milestones with meaningful rewards that align with your values and aspirations. Whether it's treating yourself to a special experience, splurging on a desired purchase, or indulging in a favorite activity, use milestone rewards as incentives to maintain momentum and motivation towards your saving goals.

Public Accountability: Share your saving milestones with friends, family, or members of your budgeting community to hold yourself publicly accountable and garner support and encouragement from others. Posting updates on social media, participating in savings challenges, or joining accountability groups can provide additional motivation and accountability to stay on track towards your financial objectives.

Reflection and Gratitude: Take time to reflect on your saving milestones and express gratitude for the progress you've made on your financial journey. Acknowledge the effort, discipline, and sacrifices that have contributed to your achievements, and cultivate a sense of gratitude for the abundance and opportunities that saving affords you in your life.

### Summary and Next Steps

Incorporating advanced saving techniques, harnessing the power of compound interest, and leveraging saving milestones are key strategies to optimize your saving potential and accelerate progress towards your financial goals. By embracing these techniques, you can enhance your financial resilience, amplify your wealth-building efforts, and achieve greater financial security and freedom.

In the following chapters, we will explore additional topics such as debt management, investment strategies, and wealth-building principles to further empower you on your journey towards financial mastery. Stay committed to your saving goals, remain flexible and adaptable in your approach, and celebrate each milestone as a testament to your financial resilience and determination.

# 4 CONQUERING DEBT: STRATEGIES FOR FINANCIAL FREEDOM

Debt can be a significant obstacle on the path to financial freedom, but with the right strategies and mindset, it is conquerable. In this chapter, we will explore effective strategies for managing and eliminating debt, empowering you to take control of your finances and achieve lasting financial freedom.

## Understanding the Impact of Debt

Before diving into debt management strategies, it's crucial to understand the impact of debt on your financial well-being. Debt comes in various forms, including credit card debt, student loans, mortgages, and personal loans, each with its own implications for your financial health.

Interest Costs: Debt accrues interest over time, increasing the total amount you owe and prolonging the time it takes to repay. High-interest debt, such as credit card debt, can accumulate rapidly, making it particularly burdensome if left unchecked.

Cash Flow Constraints: Debt payments can strain your cash flow, limiting your ability to save, invest, or pursue other financial goals. High debt-to-income ratios may restrict your financial flexibility and make it challenging to weather unexpected expenses or income disruptions.

Psychological Stress: Debt can take a toll on your mental and emotional well-being, causing stress, anxiety, and feelings of overwhelm. Constantly worrying about debt payments can detract from your quality of life and hinder your ability to focus on long-term financial planning and goal achievement.

### Creating a Debt Repayment Plan

The first step in conquering debt is to create a structured repayment plan tailored to your financial situation and goals. Consider the following steps when developing your debt repayment strategy:

Assess Your Debt: Compile a comprehensive list of all your debts, including outstanding balances, interest rates, minimum monthly payments, and repayment terms. Understanding the full scope of your debt obligations is essential for formulating an effective repayment plan.

Prioritize Debts: Prioritize your debts based on factors such as interest rates, repayment terms, and potential consequences for non-payment. High-interest debts should typically be prioritized for accelerated repayment to minimize interest costs and expedite debt elimination.

Choose a Repayment Strategy: Select a debt repayment strategy that aligns with your preferences and financial capabilities. Common approaches include the debt snowball method, which prioritizes paying off debts from smallest to largest balance, and the debt avalanche method, which focuses on tackling debts with the highest interest rates first.

Allocate Extra Funds: Allocate any extra funds, such as windfalls, bonuses, or tax refunds, towards debt repayment to accelerate progress and reduce interest costs. Consider reallocating discretionary spending from non-essential expenses towards debt reduction to free up additional funds for repayment.

### Managing Debt Wisely

In addition to implementing a structured debt repayment plan, consider adopting prudent financial practices to manage debt wisely and minimize its impact on your financial health:

Avoiding New Debt: Cease accruing new debt while actively working towards debt repayment. Exercise restraint in using credit cards or taking on additional loans, and focus on living within your means to prevent further accumulation of debt.

Negotiating Terms: Explore opportunities to negotiate with creditors or lenders for more favorable repayment terms, such as lower interest rates, extended repayment periods, or debt settlement arrangements. Open communication and willingness to collaborate may result in mutually beneficial solutions for debt resolution.

Seeking Professional Guidance: If you're struggling to manage debt on your own, consider seeking assistance from a certified credit counselor or financial advisor. These professionals can provide personalized guidance, negotiate with creditors on your behalf, and offer strategies for debt consolidation or restructuring.

Staying Committed: Stay committed to your debt repayment plan, even when faced with challenges or setbacks along the way. Consistency and perseverance are key to overcoming debt obstacles and achieving long-term financial freedom.

### Celebrating Debt-Free Milestones

As you make progress towards debt elimination, celebrate each milestone as a testament to your hard work and dedication. Whether it's paying off a credit card, eliminating a student loan, or becoming entirely debt-free, acknowledge and celebrate these achievements as significant milestones on your journey to financial freedom.

Financial Freedom Fund: Consider redirecting

funds previously allocated towards debt repayment towards building an emergency fund or investing for the future once you become debt-free. Establishing a financial freedom fund provides a financial safety net and lays the groundwork for building wealth and achieving broader financial goals.

Reflecting on Lessons Learned: Take time to reflect on the lessons learned from your debt repayment journey. Identify behaviors, habits, or decisions that contributed to debt accumulation and develop strategies to prevent similar pitfalls in the future. Use these insights to cultivate healthier financial habits and strengthen your financial resilience moving forward.

Paying It Forward: Pay it forward by sharing your debt repayment success story and insights with others who may be facing similar challenges. Offer support, encouragement, and practical guidance to inspire and empower others on their journey to debt freedom and financial empowerment.

## Leveraging Debt for Financial Growth

While debt often carries a negative connotation, it's essential to recognize that not all debt is inherently bad. When used strategically, debt can serve as a tool for financial growth and wealth accumulation. Consider the following ways to leverage debt effectively:

Investment Opportunities: Use debt to finance investment opportunities with the potential for high returns. For example, taking out a mortgage to purchase rental property or leveraging margin loans to invest in the stock market can amplify your investment returns over time, provided you carefully assess risks and exercise prudent financial management.

Business Expansion: Entrepreneurial ventures often require capital to fuel growth and expansion. Securing business loans or lines of credit can provide the necessary funding to scale operations, launch new products or services, or enter new markets. When used judiciously, debt can facilitate business growth and increase profitability.

Education and Skills Development: Invest in yourself by using student loans or educational loans to pursue higher education, professional certifications, or skills development programs. A well-chosen educational investment can lead to increased earning potential and career advancement opportunities, ultimately offsetting the cost of debt incurred.

Asset Acquisition: Finance the acquisition of appreciating assets, such as real estate or business assets, using debt. By leveraging debt to acquire income-producing assets or assets with the potential for capital appreciation, you can accelerate wealth accumulation and diversify your investment portfolio effectively.

**Refinancing and Debt Consolidation**
Refinancing and debt consolidation are strategies that can help you manage debt more effectively, reduce interest costs, and streamline repayment efforts. Consider the

following options for refinancing and debt consolidation:

Loan Refinancing: Refinance existing debt, such as high-interest credit card debt or loans, with a new loan offering more favorable terms, such as a lower interest rate or extended repayment period. Loan refinancing can lower monthly payments, reduce overall interest costs, and simplify debt management by consolidating multiple debts into a single loan.

Balance Transfer: Transfer high-interest credit card balances to a credit card offering an introductory 0% APR promotional period on balance transfers. By consolidating credit card debt onto a single card with a lower or zero interest rate, you can save on interest costs and accelerate debt repayment during the promotional period.

Debt Consolidation Loans: Obtain a debt consolidation loan to combine multiple debts into a single loan with a fixed interest rate and structured repayment plan. Debt consolidation loans can streamline debt management, lower interest costs, and simplify monthly payments, making it easier to track progress towards debt elimination.

Home Equity Loans or Lines of Credit: Tap into your home equity through a home equity loan or home equity line of credit (HELOC) to consolidate high-interest debt or finance major expenses. Home equity loans typically offer lower interest rates than unsecured debt, making them an attractive option for debt consolidation purposes.

## Avoiding Common Debt Traps

While leveraging debt can be beneficial when used strategically, it's essential to exercise caution and avoid common debt traps that can lead to financial distress. Be mindful of the following pitfalls when managing debt:

Overleveraging: Avoid overextending yourself by taking on more debt than you can comfortably afford to repay. Conduct a thorough assessment of your financial situation and borrowing capacity before taking on additional debt to ensure you can manage repayment obligations effectively.

High-Interest Debt: Beware of high-interest debt, such as payday loans, title loans, or high-interest credit cards, which can quickly spiral out of control due to exorbitant interest rates and fees. Prioritize paying off high-interest debt as quickly as possible to minimize interest costs and alleviate financial stress.

Debt for Consumption: Refrain from using debt to finance non-essential or discretionary expenses, such as luxury purchases, vacations, or entertainment. While it may be tempting to indulge in instant gratification, accumulating debt for consumption purposes can undermine long-term financial stability and delay progress towards financial goals.

Variable-Rate Debt: Exercise caution when taking on variable-rate debt, such as adjustable-rate mortgages or variable-rate loans, which are susceptible to interest rate fluctuations. Be prepared for potential interest rate increases in the future and assess your ability to afford higher payments if rates rise.

Summary and Next Steps

Debt can be a double-edged sword, offering opportunities for financial growth and wealth creation when used strategically, yet posing risks and challenges when mismanaged. By leveraging debt for financial growth, exploring refinancing and debt consolidation options, and avoiding common debt traps, you can harness the power of debt effectively while mitigating potential risks.

In the following chapters, we will delve into additional topics such as investment strategies, retirement planning, and wealth preservation techniques to further empower you on your journey towards financial mastery. Stay informed, stay vigilant, and remember that prudent debt management is a crucial aspect of achieving long-term financial success and security.

# 5 INVESTING FOR WEALTH ACCUMULATION AND FINANCIAL INDEPENDENCE

Investing is a cornerstone of wealth accumulation and financial independence, allowing individuals to grow their assets and achieve long-term financial goals. In this chapter, we will explore the fundamentals of investing, key investment principles, and strategies to help you navigate the complex world of investing effectively.

## Understanding the Basics of Investing

Before delving into specific investment strategies, it's essential to grasp the fundamental concepts and principles of investing:

Risk and Return: Every investment carries a certain level of risk, and higher-risk investments typically offer the potential for higher returns. Understanding your risk tolerance and investment horizon is crucial for selecting investments aligned with your financial goals and risk preferences.

Asset Allocation: Diversification across different asset classes, such as stocks, bonds, real estate, and alternative investments, is essential for managing risk and optimizing investment returns. Asset allocation allows you to balance risk and return based on your investment objectives and time horizon.

Time Horizon: Your investment time horizon, or the length of time you plan to hold an investment, influences your investment strategy and asset allocation decisions. Longer time horizons typically allow for more aggressive investment strategies, while shorter time horizons may require a more conservative approach to preserve capital.

Costs and Fees: Consider the impact of investment costs and fees, such as management fees, brokerage commissions, and expense ratios, on your investment returns. Minimizing costs and fees can significantly enhance your overall investment performance over time.

## Building a Diversified Investment Portfolio

Constructing a diversified investment portfolio is essential for mitigating risk and maximizing long-term returns. Consider the following principles when building your investment portfolio:

Asset Allocation: Allocate your investment capital across different asset classes based on your risk tolerance, investment objectives, and time horizon. A well-diversified portfolio typically includes a mix of stocks, bonds, cash equivalents, and alternative investments to spread risk and capture growth opportunities.

Stock Investments: Invest in a diversified portfolio of stocks to capitalize on the growth potential of equities over the long term. Consider factors such as company fundamentals, industry trends, and valuation metrics when selecting individual stocks or equity mutual funds.

Bond Investments: Incorporate fixed-income investments, such as government bonds, corporate bonds, or bond funds, into your portfolio to provide stability and income generation. Bonds offer a steady stream of interest payments and act as a buffer against stock market volatility.

Real Estate and Alternative Investments: Explore opportunities to diversify your portfolio with investments in real estate, commodities, precious metals, or other alternative assets. These assets can provide additional diversification benefits and inflation protection, enhancing overall portfolio resilience.

**Investment Strategies for Wealth Accumulation**

Once you've established a diversified investment portfolio, consider implementing the following strategies to maximize wealth accumulation and achieve your long-term financial goals:

Systematic Investing: Adopt a systematic investment approach, such as dollar-cost averaging or periodic rebalancing, to capitalize on market fluctuations and mitigate timing risk. By investing consistently over time, you can benefit from market volatility and potentially lower your average cost per share.

Long-Term Perspective: Maintain a long-term perspective when investing and avoid making impulsive decisions based on short-term market fluctuations. Focus on the underlying fundamentals of your investments and stay committed to your investment strategy through market ups and downs.

Tax-Efficient Investing: Consider tax implications when managing your investment portfolio and explore tax-efficient investment strategies, such as maximizing contributions to tax-advantaged retirement accounts, harvesting tax losses, and utilizing tax-efficient investment vehicles.

Reinvestment of Dividends and Distributions: Reinvest dividends, interest payments, and capital gains distributions back into your investment portfolio to compound returns over time. Reinvestment allows you to harness the power of compounding and accelerate wealth accumulation without incurring transaction costs.

## Monitoring and Adjusting Your Investment Portfolio

Regular monitoring and periodic adjustments are essential for maintaining the optimal performance and alignment of your investment portfolio. Consider the following practices for monitoring and managing your investments effectively:

Portfolio Rebalancing: Periodically rebalance your investment portfolio to realign asset allocations with your target allocations and risk tolerance. Rebalancing ensures that your portfolio remains diversified and aligned with your long-term investment objectives.

Performance Evaluation: Evaluate the performance of your investment portfolio regularly and compare it against relevant benchmarks or investment objectives. Identify areas of strength and weakness, analyze the factors driving performance, and make adjustments as needed to optimize portfolio returns.

Stay Informed: Stay informed about market developments, economic trends, and geopolitical events that may impact your investments. Maintain a diversified information sources and seek out reputable sources of financial news and analysis to inform your investment decisions.

Consult with Financial Professionals: Consider seeking guidance from financial professionals, such as financial advisors, investment managers, or tax professionals, to help you navigate complex investment decisions and develop a personalized investment plan customized to your own fina ncial objectives and circumstances.

## Advanced Investment Strategies

Once you've established a solid foundation in investing, consider exploring advanced strategies to further optimize your portfolio and enhance your wealth-building potential:

Sector Rotation: Implement a sector rotation strategy to capitalize on economic cycles and sector-specific trends. Rotate investments across different sectors of the economy based on macroeconomic indicators, market conditions, and sector performance. By overweighting sectors poised for growth and underweighting sectors facing headwinds, you can potentially enhance portfolio returns and minimize downside risk.

Factor Investing: Explore factor-based investing strategies that target specific characteristics or factors associated with outperformance in the market. Value, momentum, quality, and low volatilit y are common criteria. Constructing a factor-based portfolio allows you to systematically tilt towards factors that historically generate excess returns over the long term.

Tactical Asset Allocation: Employ a tactical asset allocation approach to dynamically adjust your portfolio allocations in response to changing market conditions and investment opportunities. Monitor macroeconomic indicators, technical analysis signals, and market sentiment to make timely adjustments to asset allocations and capitalize on short-term market inefficiencies.

Alternative Investments: Consider allocating a portion of your portfolio to alternative investments, such as hedge funds, private equity, venture capital, or real assets. Alternative investments offer diversification benefits, low correlation with traditional asset classes, and potential for enhanced risk-adjusted returns. However, alternative investments typically require higher minimum investments and may entail greater liquidity and regulatory risks.

Retirement Planning and Long-Term Wealth Preservation
As you progress on your investment journey, prioritize retirement planning and long-term wealth preservation to secure your financial future and achieve lasting financial independence:

Retirement Savings Strategies: Develop a comprehensive retirement savings strategy that encompasses employer-sponsored retirement plans, individual retirement accounts (IRAs), and other tax-advantaged retirement accounts. Maximize contributions to retirement accounts, take advantage of employer matching contributions, and consider implementing catch-up contributions as you approach retirement age.

Asset Protection: Safeguard your wealth and assets through effective asset protection strategies, such as insurance coverage, estate planning, and legal structures. Review your insurance policies regularly to ensure adequate coverage for life, health, disability, and property. Consult with legal and financial professionals to establish trusts, limited liability entities, or other asset protection mechanisms tailored to your specific needs and circumstances.

Estate Planning: Develop a comprehensive estate plan to outline your wishes regarding the distribution of assets, guardianship of dependents, and healthcare directives in the event of incapacity or death. Create a will, establish trusts, and designate beneficiaries for retirement accounts and life insurance policies to ensure a smooth transfer of wealth and minimize estate taxes and probate costs.

Legacy Planning: Consider incorporating philanthropy and charitable giving into your wealth preservation strategy to leave a lasting legacy and make a positive impact on society. Explore donor-advised funds, charitable trusts, or private foundations as vehicles for charitable giving and legacy planning, and involve family members in discussions about shared values and charitable objectives.

**Continuing Education and Lifelong Learning**
Finally, prioritize continuing education and lifelong learning to stay informed about evolving investment trends, financial strategies, and regulatory developments. Attend seminars, workshops, and conferences hosted by reputable financial institutions, academic institutions, or professional organizations to expand your knowledge and network with industry

experts. Stay abreast of relevant publications, research reports, and online resources to deepen your understanding of investment principles and refine your investment approach over time.

By incorporating advanced investment strategies, prioritizing retirement planning and long-term wealth preservation, and committing to lifelong learning, you can optimize your investment portfolio and achieve enduring financial success and security. In the following chapters, we will explore additional topics such as tax planning, risk management, and philanthropy to further empower you on your journey towards financial mastery. Stay curious, stay engaged, and embrace the opportunities for growth and learning that investing offers.

# 6 NAVIGATING TAX PLANNING FOR FINANCIAL EFFICIENCY

Tax planning is a crucial aspect of personal finance that can significantly impact your overall financial well-being. By understanding tax laws, optimizing tax strategies, and minimizing tax liabilities, you can enhance your financial efficiency and maximize wealth accumulation. In this chapter, we will explore key principles of tax planning and strategies to help you navigate the complex landscape of taxation effectively.

## Understanding Tax Basics

Before diving into tax planning strategies, it's essential to grasp the fundamental concepts of taxation:

Types of Taxes: Familiarize yourself with various types of taxes, including income tax, capital gains tax, dividend tax, estate tax, and property tax. Each type of tax may have different rates, deductions, and exemptions, impacting your overall tax liability.

Tax Filing Status: Determine your tax filing status based on your marital status and household composition, such as single, married filing jointly, married filing separately, or head of household. Your filing status determines your tax bracket, standard deduction, and eligibility for certain tax credits and deductions.

Taxable Income: Understand what constitutes taxable income, including wages, salaries, interest, dividends, capital gains, rental income, and other sources of income. Deductions, exemptions, and credits may reduce your taxable income, resulting in lower tax liability.

Tax Rates and Brackets: Know the applicable tax rates and brackets for different types of income and filing statuses. Tax rates may vary based on income levels, with higher-income earners typically subject to higher marginal tax rates.

## Leveraging Tax-Efficient Investment Strategies

Investing with tax efficiency in mind can help minimize tax liabilities and enhance after-tax returns. Consider the following tax-efficient investment strategies:

Tax-Advantaged Accounts: Maximize contributions to tax-advantaged retirement accounts, such as 401(k)s, IRAs, and Roth IRAs, to benefit from tax-deferred or tax-free growth. Contributions to traditional retirement accounts may be tax-deductible, while distributions from Roth accounts are tax-free in retirement.

Asset Location: Place tax-efficient investments, such as index funds or municipal bonds, in taxable brokerage accounts to minimize taxable income and capital gains. Reserve tax-inefficient investments, such as actively managed funds or high-yield bonds, for tax-advantaged retirement accounts.

Tax-Loss Harvesting: Implement tax-loss harvesting strategies to offset capital gains with capital losses and reduce taxable income. Sell investments with unrealized losses to realize losses for tax purposes while reinvesting the proceeds in similar, but not substantially identical, securities to maintain portfolio exposure.

Dividend and Interest Management: Consider the tax implications of dividends and interest income when selecting investments. Favor tax-efficient investments that generate qualified dividends or tax-exempt interest, such as municipal bonds, to minimize taxable income.

## Maximizing Tax Deductions and Credits

Explore opportunities to maximize tax deductions and credits to reduce taxable income and lower tax liabilities:

Itemized Deductions: Itemize deductions, such as mortgage interest, property taxes, charitable contributions, and medical expenses, if they exceed the standard deduction. Keep detailed records and receipts to substantiate deductible expenses and maximize tax savings.

Above-the-Line Deductions: Take advantage

of above-the-line deductions, such as contributions to retirement accounts, health savings accounts (HSAs), and self-employment expenses, to reduce adjusted gross income (AGI) and qualify for additional tax benefits.

Tax Credits: Claim tax credits, such as the Earned Income Tax Credit (EITC), Child Tax Credit, and Education Credits, to reduce tax liabilities dollar-for-dollar. Review eligibility requirements and documentation criteria to ensure eligibility for available tax credits.

Healthcare Expenses: Leverage tax-advantaged healthcare accounts, such as Flexible Spending Accounts (FSAs) and Health Savings Accounts (HSAs), to pay for qualified medical expenses with pre-tax dollars and reduce taxable income.

### Long-Term Tax Planning Strategies

Incorporate long-term tax planning strategies to optimize tax efficiency and preserve wealth over time:

Retirement Distribution Planning: Develop a tax-efficient withdrawal strategy for retirement accounts to minimize tax liabilities during retirement. Consider factors such as timing, sequencing, and distribution methods to optimize retirement income while managing tax consequences.

Estate and Gift Tax Planning: Implement estate and gift tax planning strategies to minimize estate taxes and maximize wealth transfer to heirs. Utilize tax-efficient estate planning tools, such as trusts, gifting strategies, and charitable bequests, to preserve assets and minimize tax liabilities upon transfer.

Tax-Loss Carryforwards: Utilize tax-loss carryforwards from previous years to offset capital gains and reduce taxable income in future years. Keep track of unused capital losses and carry them forward to future tax years to offset gains and mitigate tax liabilities.

Tax-Advantaged Investments: Invest in tax-advantaged vehicles, such as municipal bonds, Treasury securities, and qualified dividend-paying stocks, to generate tax-efficient income and preserve wealth over the long term. Evaluate the after-tax returns of investments and prioritize tax-efficient strategies to maximize after-tax wealth accumulation.

### Summary and Next Steps

Tax planning is a critical component of personal finance that requires careful consideration and proactive strategies to optimize financial efficiency and minimize tax liabilities. By understanding tax basics, leveraging tax-efficient investment strategies, maximizing deductions and credits, and incorporating long-term tax planning strategies, you can enhance your financial well-being and achieve lasting wealth accumulation.

In the following chapters, we will explore additional topics such as risk management, estate planning, and philanthropy to further empower you on your journey towards financial mastery. Stay informed about tax laws and regulations, consult with tax professionals as needed, and remain proactive in implementing tax-efficient strategies to achieve your financial goals.

# 7 PROTECTING YOUR WEALTH: STRATEGIES FOR RISK MANAGEMENT AND INSURANCE

Protecting your wealth is essential for safeguarding your financial security and preserving your hard-earned assets against unforeseen risks and uncertainties. In this chapter, we will explore key principles of risk management and insurance strategies to help you mitigate potential threats to your financial well-being effectively.

## Understanding Risk Management

Risk management is the process of identifying, assessing, and mitigating risks that may impact your financial stability and wealth accumulation. By adopting a proactive approach to risk management, you can minimize the adverse effects of potential threats and protect your financial interests. Consider the following principles of risk management:

Risk Identification: Identify and assess potential risks that may affect your financial situation, including market risk, inflation risk, longevity risk, health risk, disability risk, property risk, and liability risk. Conduct a comprehensive risk assessment to understand the nature and magnitude of each risk and its potential impact on your financial goals.

Risk Analysis: Evaluate the likelihood and severity of potential risks based on historical data, statistical analysis, and expert judgment. Assess the probability of occurrence and potential financial consequences associated with each risk to prioritize risk mitigation efforts effectively.

Risk Mitigation: Implement risk mitigation strategies to reduce the likelihood and impact of potential risks on your financial well-being. Explore risk transfer mechanisms, risk avoidance tactics, risk reduction measures, and risk retention strategies to manage and mitigate various types of risks effectively.

Continuous Monitoring: Regularly monitor

and review your risk management strategies to adapt to changing circumstances, emerging risks, and evolving financial goals. Stay informed about market developments, regulatory changes, and macroeconomic trends that may impact your risk exposure and adjust your risk management approach accordingly.

## Insurance Planning Essentials

Insurance plays a vital role in risk management by providing financial protection against unexpected events and potential losses. Understanding insurance basics and incorporating appropriate insurance coverage into your financial plan can help mitigate financial risks and enhance your overall financial security. Consider the following insurance planning essentials:

Health Insurance: Obtain comprehensive health insurance coverage to protect against medical expenses and healthcare costs resulting from illness, injury, or disability. Evaluate different health insurance options, including employer-sponsored plans, individual health insurance policies, and government-sponsored programs, to find the coverage that best meets your needs.

Life Insurance: Purchase life insurance coverage to provide financial support and protection for your loved ones in the event of your death. Consider factors such as your income, debt obligations, dependents' financial needs, and long-term financial goals when determining the appropriate amount and type of life insurance coverage.

Disability Insurance: Secure disability insurance coverage to replace lost income and cover living expenses if you are unable to work due to a disabling illness or injury. Choose a disability insurance policy that offers adequate benefits, a suitable waiting period, and a comprehensive definition of disability to ensure financial protection in the event of disability.

Property and Casualty Insurance: Protect your assets and belongings with property and casualty insurance coverage, including homeowners insurance, renters insurance, auto insurance, and umbrella insurance. Review policy limits, coverage options, deductibles, and exclusions to ensure adequate protection against property damage, liability claims, and other potential risks.

## Estate Planning and Asset Protection

Incorporate estate planning and asset protection strategies into your overall risk management approach to safeguard your wealth and ensure the orderly transfer of assets to future generations. Estate planning involves the creation of a comprehensive plan to manage and distribute your assets according to your wishes while minimizing taxes, probate costs, and legal complexities. Consider the following components of estate planning and asset protection:

Wills and Trusts: Prepare a will and establish trusts to outline your wishes regarding asset distribution, guardianship of minor children, and healthcare directives. A will serves as a legal document that specifies how your assets should be distributed upon your death, while trusts offer additional flexibility, privacy, and asset protection benefits.

Beneficiary Designations: Review and update beneficiary designations for retirement accounts, life insurance policies, and other financial accounts to ensure they reflect your current wishes and circumstances. Designating beneficiaries allows for the seamless transfer of assets outside of probate and minimizes potential disputes among heirs.

Asset Protection Strategies: Implement asset protection strategies, such as asset titling, gifting, asset segregation, and the use of legal entities (e.g., LLCs, partnerships, trusts), to shield your wealth from creditors, lawsuits, and other potential liabilities. Consult with legal and financial professionals to develop a customized asset protection plan tailored to your specific needs and objectives.

Long-Term Care Planning: Plan for long-term care needs and expenses by exploring options such as long-term care insurance, hybrid insurance policies, and self-funding strategies. Long-term care planning helps protect your assets and preserve your financial independence in the event of chronic illness, disability, or cognitive impairment requiring extended care.

## Implementing Risk Mitigation Strategies

Beyond insurance, there are additional risk mitigation strategies you can employ to protect your wealth and secure your financial future. These strategies aim to diversify risk, minimize exposure to potential threats, and enhance overall resilience. Let's delve deeper into these risk mitigation tactics:

### 1. Emergency Fund

Establishing an emergency fund is a foundational aspect of risk management. An emergency fund serves as a financial safety net, providing liquidity to cover unexpected expenses, such as medical bills, car repairs, or job loss, without resorting to high-interest debt or depleting long-term investments. Aim to set aside three to six months' worth of living expenses in a readily accessible savings account or money market fund to cushion against financial emergencies.

### 2. Asset Diversification

Diversifying your investment portfolio across different asset classes, industries, and geographical regions is a fundamental risk mitigation strategy. By spreading your investments across a variety of assets, you can reduce the impact of adverse market conditions or sector-specific downturns on your overall portfolio performance. Consider allocating your assets among stocks, bonds, real estate, and alternative investments to achieve a balanced and diversified investment portfolio.

3. Liability Management
Managing liabilities effectively is another critical aspect of risk mitigation. Minimize debt obligations, such as credit card debt, personal loans, or high-interest mortgages, to reduce financial leverage and interest costs. Prioritize debt repayment and adopt prudent borrowing practices to avoid excessive debt accumulation. Additionally, consider liability insurance coverage, such as umbrella insurance, to protect against potential lawsuits and legal liabilities beyond the limits of standard policies.

## 4. Contingency Planning

Developing contingency plans for potential life events, such as job loss, disability, illness, or natural disasters, can help mitigate the financial impact of unforeseen circumstances. Create a contingency budget outlining essential expenses and discretionary spending adjustments in the event of income loss or expense escalation. Consider securing disability income insurance, critical illness insurance, or business interruption insurance to provide financial support and stability during challenging times.

## 5. Education and Skill Development

Investing in education and skill development enhances your employability, earning potential, and resilience in the face of economic uncertainty. Continuously update your skills, pursue advanced certifications or professional qualifications, and diversify your expertise to adapt to evolving industry trends and job market demands. By investing in your human capital, you can increase your earning capacity and mitigate the risk of income loss or career stagnation.

## 6. Legal and Tax Compliance

Adhering to legal and tax regulations is essential for minimizing legal risks and tax liabilities. Stay informed about relevant laws, regulations, and compliance requirements governing your financial activities, investments, and business operations. Consult with legal and tax professionals to ensure compliance with applicable laws and optimize tax planning strategies to minimize tax exposure and maximize tax efficiency.

## Conclusion

Implementing risk mitigation strategies is essential for protecting your wealth, preserving financial stability, and achieving long-term financial success. By establishing emergency funds, diversifying investments, managing liabilities, developing contingency plans, investing in education, and ensuring legal and tax compliance, you can enhance your financial resilience and weather potential challenges with confidence. Continuously assess your risk exposure, adapt your risk management strategies to changing circumstances, and remain proactive in safeguarding your financial well-being. In the following chapters, we will explore additional topics such as retirement planning, investment strategies, and charitable giving to further empower you on your journey towards financial mastery. Stay vigilant, stay informed, and take proactive steps to mitigate risks and seize opportunities for financial growth and prosperity.

# 8 PLANNING FOR RETIREMENT: STRATEGIES FOR FINANCIAL INDEPENDENCE

Retirement planning is a crucial aspect of personal finance that requires careful consideration, strategic foresight, and disciplined saving and investing. Whether retirement is decades away or just around the corner, developing a comprehensive retirement plan is essential for achieving financial independence and enjoying a fulfilling post-career life. In this chapter, we will explore key principles of retirement planning and strategies to help you build a robust retirement nest egg and secure your financial future.

## Setting Retirement Goals
Before diving into retirement planning strategies, it's essential to clarify your retirement goals, aspirations, and lifestyle

preferences. Consider the following questions to define your retirement vision:

Retirement Age: At what age do you envision retiring from full-time employment and transitioning into retirement?

Lifestyle Expectations: What type of lifestyle do you envision in retirement? Will you pursue travel, hobbies, volunteer work, or other leisure activities?

Retirement Income Needs: How much income will you need in retirement to maintain your desired lifestyle and cover essential expenses?

Healthcare and Long-Term Care: Have you factored in healthcare costs and long-term care needs into your retirement budget?

By establishing clear retirement goals and objectives, you can develop a personalized retirement plan tailored to your unique financial situation and aspirations.

Assessing Retirement Readiness
Once you've defined your retirement goals,

assess your current financial situation and retirement readiness to identify any gaps or areas for improvement. Consider the following factors when evaluating your retirement preparedness:

Retirement Savings: Evaluate your retirement savings accounts, such as 401(k) plans, IRAs, and other retirement accounts, to determine if you're on track to meet your retirement income needs.

Debt and Expenses: Review your current debt obligations, living expenses, and budgeting habits to identify opportunities for debt reduction and expense optimization.

Investment Portfolio: Assess the performance and asset allocation of your investment portfolio to ensure alignment with your retirement goals, risk tolerance, and time horizon.

Social Security and Pension Benefits: Estimate your projected Social Security benefits and any pension income you may receive in retirement to supplement your retirement savings.

By conducting a comprehensive retirement readiness assessment, you can identify potential areas of improvement and take proactive steps to enhance your retirement prospects.

**Retirement Income Strategies**

Developing a sustainable retirement income strategy is essential for generating reliable income streams throughout your retirement years. Consider the following retirement income strategies to maximize income and minimize longevity risk:

Systematic Withdrawal Approach: Implement a systematic withdrawal approach, such as the 4% rule or a dynamic withdrawal strategy, to withdraw funds from your retirement accounts systematically while preserving capital and adjusting for inflation.

Guaranteed Income Products: Consider purchasing annuities or other guaranteed income products to provide a steady stream of income in retirement and mitigate longevity risk. Evaluate different annuity options, such as immediate annuities, deferred annuities, or hybrid annuities, to determine the most suitable solution for your needs.

Portfolio Diversification: Maintain a diversified investment portfolio comprising stocks, bonds, real estate, and other asset classes to generate income and mitigate investment risk. Rebalance your portfolio periodically to ensure alignment with your retirement income needs and risk tolerance.

Part-Time Employment: Explore opportunities for part-time employment or freelance work in retirement to supplement your retirement income and stay engaged in meaningful activities. Consider phased retirement options or encore career opportunities that align with your skills, interests, and lifestyle preferences.

Healthcare and Long-Term Care Planning
Factor healthcare costs and long-term care needs into your retirement plan to ensure comprehensive financial protection and peace of mind. Consider the following healthcare and long-term care planning strategies:

Health Insurance Coverage: Evaluate your

healthcare insurance options, including Medicare, supplemental insurance, and long-term care insurance, to provide comprehensive coverage for medical expenses and long-term care needs in retirement.

Health Savings Accounts (HSAs): Maximize contributions to HSAs to save for qualified medical expenses on a tax-advantaged basis and supplement Medicare coverage in retirement.

Long-Term Care Insurance: Consider purchasing long-term care insurance to protect against the potentially high costs of long-term care services, such as nursing home care, assisted living facilities, or home health care, in retirement.

Health and Wellness: Prioritize preventive healthcare measures, healthy lifestyle choices, and wellness activities to maintain optimal health and minimize healthcare expenses in retirement.

**Legacy and Estate Planning**
Finally, incorporate legacy and estate planning considerations into your retirement plan to

ensure the orderly transfer of assets and protect your wealth for future generations. Consider the following estate planning strategies:

Wills and Trusts: Prepare a will and establish trusts to outline your wishes regarding asset distribution, guardianship of minor children, and healthcare directives in retirement.

Beneficiary Designations: Review and update beneficiary designations for retirement accounts, life insurance policies, and other financial assets to ensure they align with your estate planning objectives.

Tax Planning: Minimize estate taxes and maximize wealth transfer by implementing tax-efficient estate planning strategies, such as gifting, charitable giving, and estate tax exemptions.

Legacy Planning: Incorporate philanthropy and charitable giving into your retirement plan to leave a lasting legacy and make a positive impact on causes and organizations you care about.

**Maximizing Retirement Savings**

In addition to establishing a retirement plan, maximizing retirement savings is crucial for achieving your financial goals. Consider the following strategies to boost your retirement savings:

Maximize Contributions: Take advantage of employer-sponsored retirement plans, such as 401(k)s or 403(b)s, and contribute the maximum allowable amount each year. If you're self-employed, consider setting up a solo 401(k) or SEP IRA to maximize retirement contributions.

Catch-Up Contributions: If you're age 50 or older, take advantage of catch-up contributions to turbocharge your retirement savings. Catch-up contributions allow individuals to contribute additional funds to their retirement accounts beyond the standard limits, helping them make up for lost time and accelerate savings growth.

Automate Savings: Set up automatic contributions to your retirement accounts to ensure consistent and disciplined savings. By automating your savings, you can make retirement contributions a priority and avoid the temptation to spend money earmarked for retirement on other expenses.

Reduce Expenses: Identify areas where you can trim expenses and redirect savings toward retirement contributions. Cut unnecessary expenses, negotiate lower bills, and prioritize saving for retirement to boost your retirement savings rate.

Conclusion: Securing Your Retirement Future
Planning for retirement is a lifelong journey that requires careful consideration, strategic planning, and disciplined execution. By setting clear retirement goals, assessing your financial readiness, developing a comprehensive retirement plan, maximizing retirement savings, and implementing sound investment and income strategies, you can secure your retirement future and enjoy a fulfilling and

financially secure post-career life.

Remember that retirement planning is not a one-time event but an ongoing process that requires regular review and adjustment. Monitor your progress toward your retirement goals, adapt to changing circumstances, and seek guidance from financial professionals as needed to ensure your retirement plan remains on track.

As you embark on your retirement journey, prioritize financial discipline, prudent decision-making, and long-term vision. Stay informed about retirement planning options, stay proactive in managing your retirement savings and investments, and stay committed to achieving your retirement dreams.

# ABOUT THE AUTHOR

Vana Hendy  is a seasoned wordsmith with a passion for storytelling that has captivated readers around the world. Born and raised in Nigeria, Vana Hendy  discovered the magic of words at an early age, weaving tales that transported readers to fantastical realms and stirred their imaginations.

With a degree in Marketing  from Coal City University  , Vana Hendy combines a strongacademic foundation with a natural flair for creative expression. This unique blend of knowledge and creativity is evident in herability to craft narratives that are both intellectually stimulating and emotionally resonant.

Vana Hendy has a diverse literary palette, having penned works spanning various genres, from gripping mystery novels to heartwarming romance stories. she  believes in the transformative power of storytelling, using words to inspire, entertain, and provoke thought.